Where Does the Mail Go?

A Book about the Postal System

By Melvin and Gilda Berger
Illustrated by Geoffrey Brittingham

Ideals Children's Books • Nashville, Tennessee

The authors, artist, and publisher wish to thank the following for their invaluable advice and instruction for this book:

Jane Hyman, B.S., M. Ed. (Reading), M. Ed. (Special Needs), Ed. D. (candidate)

Rose Feinberg, B.S., M. Ed. (Elementary Education), Ed. D. (Reading and Language Arts)

Margot Myers of the United States Postal Service

R.L. 2.3 Spache

Published by Ideals Children's Books
An imprint of Hambleton-Hill Publishing, Inc.
Nashville, Tennessee 37218

Printed and bound in the United States of America

Library of Congress Cataloging-in-Publication Data
Berger, Melvin.
    Where does the mail go? : a book about the postal system / by Melvin and
Gilda Berger ; illustrated by Geoffrey H. Brittingham.
        p.   cm.—(Discovery readers)
    Includes index.
    ISBN 1-57102-022-5 (lib. bdg.)—ISBN 1-57102-006-3 (paper)
    1. Postal service—United States —Juvenile literature. [1. Postal service.] I.
Berger, Gilda. II. Brittingham, Geoffrey, ill. III. Title. IV. Series.
HE6371.B36   1994
383'.4973—dc20   94-6254
                                                                                                    CIP
                                                                                                    AC

Where Does the Mail Go? is part of the *Discovery Readers*™ series.
Discovery Readers is a trademark of Hambleton-Hill Publishing, Inc.

Where does the mail go?
Just mail a letter and see.
Matty did.
And this is what happened.

Matty dropped his letter into the
    mailbox.
He read the card on the box.
He saw that the next pickup would
    be at one in the afternoon.
Matty decided to wait.

Soon it was one o'clock.
A mail truck pulled up.
Out stepped the letter carrier.
Her name was Linda.
She carried a key and an empty carton.

Linda unlocked the mailbox.
She opened the mailbox door.
Lots of letters were piled up inside.
Linda tossed all of them into the carton.
She locked the mailbox.

Linda put the carton into her truck.
And away she drove.
Goodbye, letter, thought Matty.
I wonder what happens now?

Linda stopped at other mailboxes.
She filled more cartons with letters.
Finally, she drove to the post office.

7

Linda carried the cartons inside.
Other letter carriers were there.
They were placing mail in trays.
Linda did the same.
Can you see Matty's letter?

Other workers took the trays.
They piled them into carts.
Then they wheeled the carts out to a
    big truck.
Where is Matty's letter now?

Finally, all the mail was in the truck.
Mitch, the driver, climbed in.
He pulled the big truck away from
    the post office.

Mitch drove to another post office.
He picked up more carts.
He filled the big truck with carts.

Then Mitch drove to a postal center.
The United States has about 350
    postal centers.
Each one collects mail from many
    post offices.

Mail handlers work in the postal
    centers.
They dump the letters into a large
    bin.
The bin is part of a large machine.

This machine sorts the mail.
It pulls out packages.
And it pulls out extra-big envelopes.
Letters like Matty's pass right
    through.
Can you find Matty's letter?

control panel

13

The letters go to the next machine.
This one does many jobs.

It looks at each letter and finds the
  stamp.
It turns all the letters to face the
  same way.

It prints wavy lines on the stamp.
These lines cancel the stamp.
Now the stamp cannot be used
again.

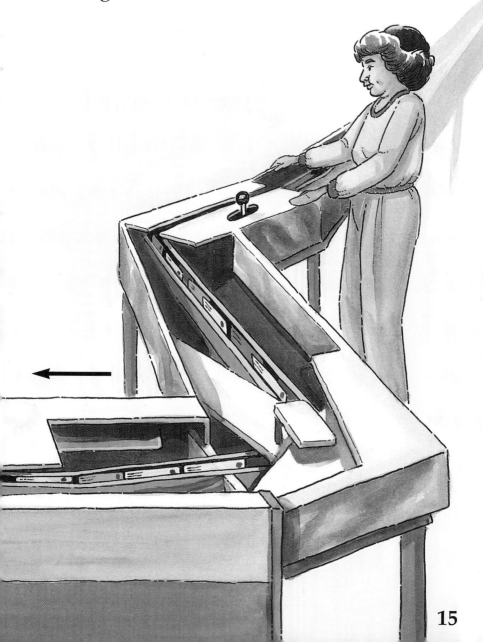

The machine also prints the
postmark on the envelope.
The postmark shows:

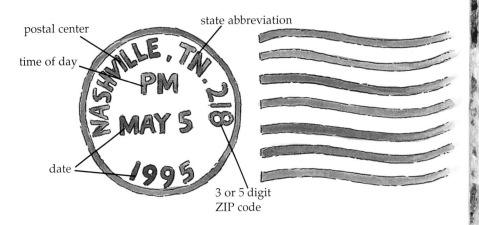

postal center
time of day
state abbreviation
date
3 or 5 digit
ZIP code

The machine then separates the letters.
Letters with addresses written by
hand go one way.
Letters with printed addresses go
another way.

Matty used a typewriter to print his
letter.
He also used it to print the address on
the envelope.
His letter goes with the printed
addresses.

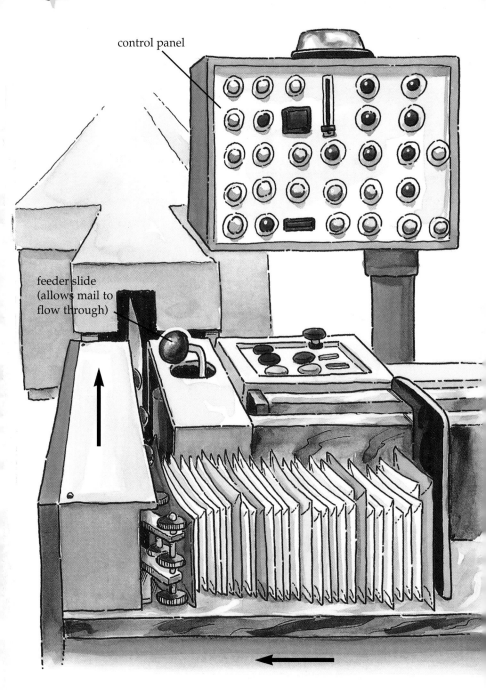

control panel

feeder slide
(allows mail to
flow through)

Another machine now takes over.
This one has two main jobs.

17

It reads the ZIP code.
The ZIP code is a special number.
It tells where the letter is going.

backer plate
(holds letters
in place)

The machine also prints a row of
    lines on the envelope.
These lines are called a bar code.
The bar code takes the place of the
    ZIP code.

United States Postal Service
Stamp Services
475 L'Enfant Plaza SW
Washington, DC 20260-2439

Finally, the letters reach the last
   machine.
This one reads the bar codes.
Snap!
It drops each letter into a certain bin.
Each bin has its own code number.

bin

tray

What happens to the letters with
addresses written by hand?
They go to other machine operators.
The operators read the ZIP codes on
the letters.
They punch the numbers into the
machine.
The letters go into bins.

Workers take the letters from each
   bin.
They put them into trays.
All the letters in a tray go to the
   same area.

Workers put a label on each tray.
The bar-coded label gives the first
   three numbers of the ZIP code.
All ZIP codes that start with 202 go
   to Washington, D.C.
Matty's letter goes into that tray.
Where is Matty's letter?

Some trays go into one truck.
This mail is not going very far.
The truck goes to nearby post
offices.

Some trays go into a different truck.
This mail is going more than 200
miles away.
This truck goes to an airport.
Matty's letter goes in this truck.

The truck goes to the airport.
Workers load the mail on an airplane.
The airplane flies to Washington, D.C.

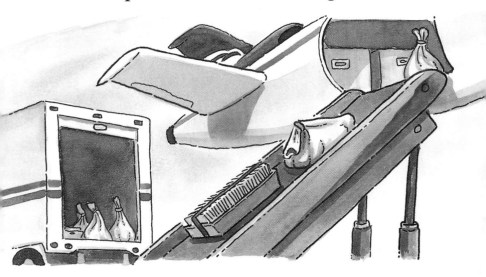

Trucks are waiting at the airport.
Their drivers pick up the mail.
They drive the letters to another
    postal center.

A machine sorts the letters by ZIP code.
Letters with the same ZIP code go into the same bin.

Workers pick up the bins.
They load them into trucks.
Each bin goes to a different post office.

Most ZIP codes cover many streets.
Lots of people live in each ZIP code area.
Lots of stores and offices are there too.

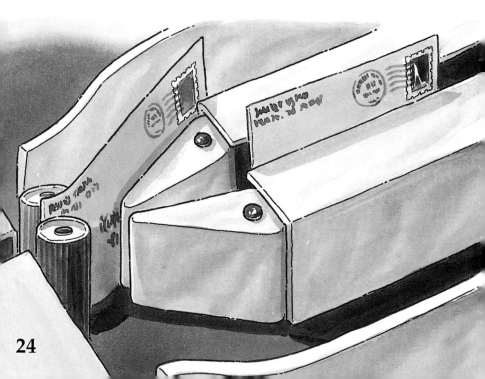

Tom and Sally are letter carriers at a
    post office.
They take the letters.
They sort them by street and
    number.
And they put all the letters in order.

Tom takes mail to buildings that are
   far apart.
He drives a post office truck.
He drives from house to house.
He puts the letters in the mailboxes.
Sometimes he parks and walks.
Then he drives again.

Sally takes mail to buildings that are
    close together.
She puts the mail into a big bag.
She walks from place to place.
She leaves mail at the desks in office
    buildings.

Matty's letter has ZIP code
20260-2439.

20260 is the ZIP code for just one
building.

2439 is the code for one department
in this building.

What building is it?

It is the main office of the U.S. Postal
Service.

Its full address is:

U.S. Postal Service
475 L'Enfant Plaza
Washington, DC 20260

People send stacks of letters to the
U.S. Postal Service every day.

The mail is too much for one letter
carrier.

So the mail goes by truck to this
building.

475

UNITED STATES POSTAL SERVICE

29

Workers take the mail out of the
    truck.
They put the letters into carts.
And they wheel the carts to offices
    in the building.

Matty's letter goes to a special
 office.
It is the office for stamp collecting.
Can you spot Matty's letter?

Nancy works in this office.
She opens Matty's letter.
And she reads:

Dear U.S. Postal Service,

Please send me your free
booklet, *Introduction to Stamp
Collecting.*

My address is:

1501 County Hospital Road
Nashville, TN 37218

Thank you.

Matty Miller

Nancy takes a booklet off the shelf.
She puts it in an envelope.
She addresses the envelope.

And she mails it to Matty.

Matty checks the mail every day.
Nothing comes for about a week.
Finally, he spots a big envelope.

Matty tears it open.
He reads through the booklet.
Stamp collecting looks like fun,
    Matty thinks.
But it might be even more fun with
    a friend.
I'll ask Sara.

Matty thinks of sending Sara a letter
   by Express Mail.
The letter would arrive the next day.

Priority Mail would be a little
   slower.
The letter would take about two days.

Matty could also call Sara on the
telephone.
But he decides to use a facsimile
machine.
This is also called a fax machine.
It uses computers and telephone
wires to send a printed message.

Matty writes a letter.
He puts the letter into the fax
machine.
Matty dials Sara's fax machine
number.

Zip!
The message flashes through the
    telephone wires.
Zap!
Sara gets a copy of Matty's letter.

Sara faxes back her reply.
"Sure. Let's collect stamps.
"I'll write for the booklet too.
"Thank you for the address."

Stamp collecting in the United
    States is a very old hobby.
It began in 1847.
That's when the United States sold
    its first stamps.

All countries sell stamps.
The money pays for mail delivery.
The stamps have different values.

Stamps that cost more go on letters
that weigh more.

They also go on letters to other
countries.

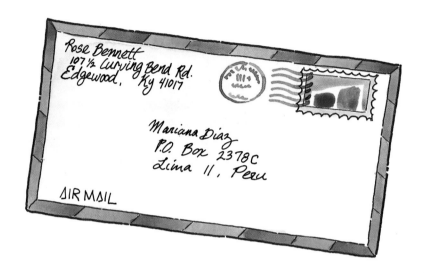

Stamps that cost less go on postcards.

People collect stamps for many
reasons.

Some like stamps that are very old.

Some like stamps that are brand-new.

Some like stamps that show famous
people.

Some like stamps that show animals.

Most people find out about stamps
from books.

They trade stamps.

They sell them to other people.

You can collect stamps too.
Write to the U.S. Postal Service.
Put your name and address on the
letter.
Ask for the booklet *Introduction to
Stamp Collecting.*

Put the letter in an envelope.
Address the envelope to:

U.S. Postal Service
Stamp Services
475 L'Enfant Plaza S.W.
Washington, DC 20260-2439

Glue a stamp on the envelope.
And drop the letter into a mailbox.

Your letter will go
—to the post office

—to a postal center

—through different machines

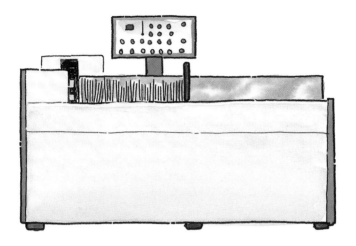

—into a bin

—onto an airplane or truck

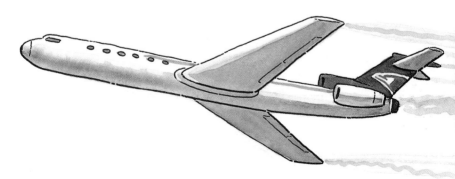

—to another postal center

—to the stamp collecting
   department in the U.S. Postal
   Service.

Where does the mail go?
Just mail a letter and see!

Index